New from Old: Recycling Plastic

Written by Anthony Robinson

Contents

Collins

What is recycling?

Recycling is making something new from something that has already been used.

Instead of throwing things away we can collect and recycle them to make new things.

What can we recycle?

We can recycle glass, metal, plastic and paper.

glass

metal

plastic

paper

4

Let's look at plastic. We use it every day.
Only some kinds of plastic are easy to recycle.
Some plastic is hard to recycle.

easy to recycle

hard to recycle

How do we recycle plastic?

First we collect the plastic.

It is sorted into different kinds.

Then it is cut into small bits and washed.

After it has been washed, the plastic is melted and made into pellets. Now the old plastic can be used again.

New things we can make

We can make many things out of recycled plastic.

clothes

furniture

toys

11

Why is it good to recycle?

Too much rubbish is
bad for the planet.

What can we do? We can reduce how much we use. We can reuse things. And we can recycle.

How plastic is recycled

Put it in the recycling bin.

Collect the plastic.

Make something new from the pellets.

Turn it into pellets.

Sort it.

Cut it.

Wash it.

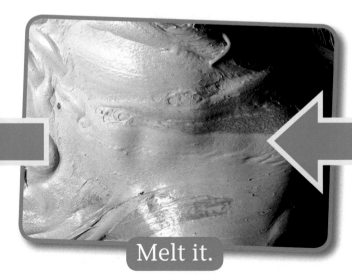

Melt it.

15

Ideas for reading

Written by Clare Dowdall PhD
Lecturer and Primary Literacy Consultant

Learning objectives: apply phonic knowledge and skills as the prime approach to reading unfamiliar words that are not completely decodable; use syntax and context when reading for meaning; find specific information in simple texts; recognise the main elements that shape different texts; take turns to speak, listen to each other's suggestions and talk about what they are going to do

Curriculum links: Geography: Improving the environment

High frequency words: new, from, old, do, out, what, be, good, how, make, that, has, been, them, some, first, then, after, now, again, many, too, much

Interest words: recycling, plastic, recycle, reuse, glass, metal, paper, pellets, clothes, furniture, toys, planet, reduce

Resources: whiteboard, pieces of plastic, paper and metal, flash cards for interest words

Word count: 149

Getting started

- Look at the front cover with the children. Explain that this book is about recycling plastic and check that the children understand what recycling is.

- Sort some items into three sets: plastic, paper and metal. Check that children can identify plastic materials.

- Read the title and blurb with the children. Focus on the words *recycle* and *reuse*. Help children to read them by breaking them into constituent syllables and using phonic cues.

- Discuss and identify the features of this information book, e.g. labels, photographs, diagrams.

Reading and responding

- Look at the contents list together. Read it aloud and model how to use it to find specific information.

- Discuss whether this is a book that should be read in order, or whether children can select information that interests them.